Turkey and the New States of the Caucasus and Central Asia

Bülent Gökay

Richard Langhorne

January 1996

Wilton Park Paper 111

Report based on Wilton Park Conference 448: 18–22 September 1995: "Turkey, the Caucasus and the Central Asian Republics" in association with the Turkish International Cooperation Agency (TICA), Ankara.

London: HMSO

ISBN 0 11 701522 9
ISSN 0953 8542

Published by HMSO and available from:

HMSO Publications Centre
(Mail, fax and telephone orders only)
PO Box 276, London SW8 5DT
Telephone orders 0171 873 9090
General enquiries 0171 873 0011
(queuing system in operation for both numbers)
Fax orders 0171 873 8200

HMSO Bookshops
49 High Holborn, London WC1V 6HB
(counter service only)
0171 873 0011 Fax 0171 831 1326
68–69 Bull Street, Birmingham B4 6AD
0121 236 9696 Fax 0121 236 9699
33 Wine Street, Bristol BS1 2BQ
0117 926 4306 Fax 0117 929 4515
9–21 Princess Street, Manchester M60 8AS
0161 834 7201 Fax 0161 833 0634
16 Arthur Street, Belfast BT1 4GD
01232 238451 Fax 01232 235401
71 Lothian Road, Edinburgh EH3 9AZ
0131 228 4181 Fax 0131 229 2734
The HMSO Oriel Bookshop
The Friary, Cardiff CF1 4AA
01222 395548 Fax 01222 384347

HMSO's Accredited Agents
(see Yellow Pages)

and through good booksellers

Contents

1   Introduction

The end of the Cold War and the collapse of the Soviet Union have changed the balance of power in the vast lands of Eurasia, creating historic opportunities and dangers at the same time. On the one hand, the abandonment of authoritarian systems and the democratisation of politics within the states of the former Soviet Union have improved the possibility of global co-operation and transcended the enmities of the Cold War. On the other, acute instability within the new states and growing tension among them have created a serious risk of interstate clashes and widespread civil war in the heart of Eurasia.

These radical changes have profoundly affected the international configuration of power. The bipolarity that dominated the international system from 1945 to 1991 is now history. A changed geopolitical environment and the new distribution of forces have invited new actors to the region. Turkey is one of those external actors. The collapse of the Soviet Union and the subsequent emergence of the new independent states in Central Asia and the Caucasus have presented Turkey with a host of challenges and opportunities unprecedented in the contemporary history of its foreign policy. While the traditional focus of Turkey's foreign policy has always been a western thrust, the new northern tier openings in the Caucasus and Central Asia have presented Turkey with significant new political spaces and have opened up possibilities for wider influence and economic and cultural expansion.

These new opportunities are nevertheless accompanied by equally significant challenges and vulnerabilities. The comfort and certainty which came with secure borders with the Soviet Union have now been replaced by considerable anxiety over the implications of regional dynamics and conflicts.

Initial Reaction

The collapse of the Soviet Union relieved Turkey at one stroke from the threat of both the military presence of a superpower and the ideological challenge of Communism. For about two centuries, Turkey's geopolitical strategy had been determined by the threat of Russian/Soviet expansionism and its particular effect on Turkey's northern and most vulnerable border.

When the Soviet Union collapsed and the republics began peeking out from behind the proverbial Iron Curtain, Turkey's relations with the independent states of these regions developed swiftly in an apparent state of euphoria upon the discovery of linguistic and religious kinship with the Central Asians and Caucasians. Bilateral cultural and economic agreements were signed with each republic, and the Turkish government rushed to recognise all of the republics when they gained independence in the autumn of 1991. Diplomatic activity seemed to become almost compulsive. Turkey initiated high-level contacts which were immediately followed by summits of the heads of the states, prime minister's and ministerial visits, non-governmental organisational contacts, private sector co-operation and collaborations. It seemed accepted that Turkey was the natural link and the obvious choice between Central Asia and the Caucasus and the rest of the world.

Initially, Turkey's position was considered as at a distinct advantage in its relations with Central Asian and the Caucasian states. It was ethnically and linguistically related to the Azeris and the inhabitants of the Central Asian republics, except the Tajiks. It shared with many of them adherence to the Sunni branch of Islam. In addition, Turkey prided itself on the secular nature of its political system. Finally, Turkey could boast of a successfully developing economy.

The period of euphoria gave rise to all kinds of claims, assumptions and speculations in Turkey and the region. It was assumed that the ethnic and linguistic kinship was so strong that Anatolian Turkish could easily be understood throughout Central Asia. For many Turks, this represented a chance to recapture the greatness of their distant past. The Central Asian and the Caucasian Muslims, for their part, seemed only to feed the Turkish feelings of euphoria. After centuries of Russian

2

colonisation and decades of Soviet totalitarian control, they were sufficiently carried away to accept the enthusiastic attention from Turkey. Probably, on a more important and more pragmatic level, the Muslims of Central Asia and the Caucasus were optimistic about the practical and particularly economic aspects of Turkey's attention.

'Turkic World': Origins of the Turkic Peoples

The scholarly consensus suggests that the first people to be known as the Turks emerged in the sixth century from the Altai Mountains.[1] The Turkic tribes who first occupied the settled areas of Central Asia were from the Oghuz tribe. As other Turkic tribes from farther east moved into Central Asia, the Oghuz moved west. This process eventually produced three famous Turkic peoples: the Khalji, the Selchuk, and the Osmanli.

The Selchuk brand of the Oghuz pressed into Khorasan in northern Iran, moved into Baghdad, and conquered much of Anatolia. This can be seen as the beginning of what would prove to be the permanent Turkification of Anatolia. In the fourteenth century, a Turkish khan from the Osman tribe established the hereditary line of the house of Osman. The western migrations of Turkic tribes ended about this time and the Osmanlis built the Ottoman Empire. By the beginning of the fifteenth century, Anatolia was fully in Ottoman control.

Meanwhile in Central Asia, after the Oghuz tribes moved west, the Turkic and Persian tribes endured centuries of invasions from east and the northeast. A Chinese tribe called Kara Kitai left considerable Chinese influence in the regions of Central Asia in this period. Before the thirteenth century Mongol invasion a group of Turkic tribes, called Kipchak, held power on the northern steppes of Central Asia. The Kipchak formed one of the main ethnic components of eastern Turkic tribes, such as Uzbek and Kazakh. The Oghuz tribes who migrated west

---

[1] Karl H. Menges, *Introduction to Turkic Studies*, New York, 1962, pp.24–27.

centuries earlier did not incorporate these Kara Kitai/Chinese and Kipchak/eastern Turkic elements.

One of the most famous events in the history of the region was the invasion by Mongol leader Cengiz Khan at the beginning of the thirteenth century. During this period, there was a relatively rapid mixing of population. Mongol ethnic influence on the Central Asians was significant. At the end of the fifteenth century, an eastern Turkic tribe, the Uzbeks, moved south from Siberia. They brought back the dominance of the eastern Turkic tradition to the region after the Mongol invasion. The rule of the Uzbeks lasted until the mid-seventeenth century.

Meanwhile in the Ottoman Empire, the Oghuz Turks who migrated to Anatolia mixed with Balkan peoples, Greeks, Bulgarians and Serbs. In this way, the Mediterranean influence became the dominant aspect of the Oghuz Turks' ethnic make-up. Thus, the ethnic and anthropological distinctions between the western Turks of Anatolia and the eastern Turks of Central Asia diverged centuries ago. In addition to their diverse and different ethnic development, the historical experiences of the Central Asian and Anatolian peoples for centuries overlapped very little.

Despite this divergence, the late nineteenth century witnessed the development of a movement known as 'pan-Turkism'. Pan-Turkism promoted the unity of the Turkic peoples of the Ottoman and Russian empires. During the second decade of the twentieth century, it became the battle cry of several Young Turk leaders who had a common concern to save the empire from dismemberment after the First World War. After the disintegration of the Ottoman Empire, the pan-Turkist movement lost its prime impetus. The Turkish national independence movement, under the leadership of Mustafa Kemal, resolutely rejected all pan-Turkist aspirations.

Mustafa Kemal's strict territorial definition of Turkey and his firm rejection of pan-Turkism virtually brought to an end all adventures and engagements outside Anatolia. With the establishment of the republic, the focus of the country shifted away from empire to nation-state. Mustafa Kemal aimed to root self-respect in specifically Anatolian Turkish national identity. Atatürk's rejection of all forms of pan-Turkism combined with a refusal to become involved in any way in the fate of other ethnic Turkic groups outside the frontiers of the republic. The foreign policy orientation of the Turkish Republic was turned toward Europe.

For most of their pre-modern and modern history, Turkey and Central Asia have essentially had no relationship. This state of affairs, however, changed radically in the late 1980s. With the demise of the Soviet Union Turkey seemed literally to pounce on the Central Asian and Transcaucasian Muslim/Turkic republics, jumping over the centuries of long separation.

2 The Political Scene: Ethnicity and Power Relations

History

Although never unified under a single state, those Central Asian regions of the former Soviet Union once in the very distant past belonged to a common Islamic civilisation that encompassed portions of modern-day Turkey, Iran, Afghanistan, Pakistan, India, Sinkiang, the Caucasus, and the Volga region. For many centuries the vast territories of Central Asia served as a launching point for nomadic invaders. Central Asia was "the reservoir holding a sea of peoples who, organised into great confederations, from time to time conquered the Middle East and China . . . From the second millennium BC to the eighteenth century the history of the region may be told in terms of ever repeated nomadic conquests, the formation of empires over oasis and settled populations, and the constant tension between pastoral and agricultural peoples".[2]

After the fourteenth century the Central Asian empires began to undergo a process of political fragmentation that gradually undermined their military power. It was in this period that Tsarist Russia began to expand eastward and to exert increasing pressure on the Tatars, Kazakhs, Uzbeks, and other Central Asian peoples. During the sixteenth and seventeenth centuries Russians expanded primarily eastward, moving through the forested northern territories of Eurasia and conquering such relatively accessible centres of Islamic influence as Tatar, Kazan and Astrakhan. Starting in the eighteenth century, Russian expansion turned southward to the regions north of the Black, Caspian, and Aral seas. Pushing farther south into the 'non-steppe' territories during the mid-nineteenth century, Russian forces took control of the Khanates of Khiva and Kokand, the emirate of Bukhara, and the remainder of Central Asia. By the 1860s, Russian generals also wrested control of much of the Caucasus from the Ottoman Sultan and the Persian Shah.

Russian expansion into Central Asia and the Caucasus provoked intense military resistance from some of the native peoples. The Kazakh population resisted for nearly sixty years. The Tsarist conquest of Bukhara and the Central Asian Khanates was also accompanied by strong resistance. In the north Caucasus, Russian expansion met stubborn resistance from Chechens and the peoples of Daghestan led by Shamil.

One circumstance that helped spark the Central Asian uprisings was the wave of Russian settlers migrating to various parts of Central Asia. In Kazakhstan more than a million people from European portions of Russia came and settled as farmers during the first decade of the twentieth century. During the Soviet era the pressure of migration continued. This population movement did not affect all of Central Asia equally. The influx of outsiders had a much stronger impact in Kazakhstan than in Uzbekistan and Tajikistan. Nonetheless, large numbers of Russian settlers had an enduring impact on all the republics along the southern border.

---

[2] I. Lapidus, *A History of Islamic Societies*, New York, 1988, p.415.

The impact of the Soviet regime on the region was greater still. Stalin's drive to reconstruct the economies of Central Asia had a disastrous effect on the lives of the local peoples. Kazakhstan was a prime target of Stalin's drive to collectivise agriculture. Resistance to this campaign was widespread among Kazakhs. As a result of collectivisation, as many as 1.5 million Kazakhs perished. Kazakhstan suffered further under Khrushchev's ambitious 'Virgin Lands' campaign of agricultural expansion. Under Stalin's rule, the Kyrgyz population suffered too. 'Russiafication' began on an enormous scale. The aim was to make Kyrgyzstan a dependable source of cheap raw materials. The party's ranks of native Kyrgyz were systematically purged and replaced by Russians. Until 1991 heirs of the Russian settlers effectively controlled the ruling Communist Party in Kyrgyzstan. Similar to the other areas of Central Asia, Stalin's collectivisation provoked strong resistance among the Tajiks. During and after the Second World War, Stalin forcibly exiled large numbers of Volga Germans from the Volga-German Autonomous Republic and Tatars from the Crimea and the North Caucasus to Tajikistan. In Turkmenistan, too, the local population violently resisted forced collectivisation of agriculture. The Soviet authorities responded with mass arrests and deportations. As a result of these campaigns, massive collective farms and irrigation schemes made a lasting impact on the traditional nomadic Turkmen life.

During the Soviet period, differences and tensions among the Central Asian peoples had been displayed in the creation of the new national republics. Soviet leadership aimed to create national republics that could counteract loyalties to long-existing entities like Bukhara or to any supranational pan-Turkic or pan-Islamic tendency. Republican boundaries had been intentionally designed to divide some large ethnic groups between two or more republics. This scheme had been implemented to undercut the political cohesion of each new national structure.

The Soviet division of Central Asia into separate national republics created a number of internal border disputes among the new political units. For almost seventy years the concentration of political power in Moscow suppressed most of these disputes, but many of them have resurfaced in the wake of Soviet Union's disintegration. For example, Kyrgyzstan is involved in a serious dispute with Tajikistan concerning the border zone in the Badken region and Isfara. The border between Kyrgyzstan's Talas region and Kazakhstan's Zhembyl region also has stirred up quarrels.

The new states of the Caucasus are also heirs to a turbulent historical legacy. Because of their relatively small size and the tensions among them, the Caucasian nations have often sought outside alliances rather than to band together. In the past, the entire region was devastated by Turkic and Mongol invasions. In the sixteenth century, a protracted and destructive struggle between the Ottoman and Persian empires occupied the area. Tsarist Russian forces first appeared in the Transcaucasian region at the end of the 18th century. By 1828, Moscow took possession of present-day Armenia.

In April 1918, witnessing the dissolution of the Tsarist Empire and taking advantage of fragmented Bolshevik power, Transcaucasian nations declared their independence and established the Transcaucasian Federated Republic. A month later this union dissolved as Azerbaijan, Armenia and Georgia moved to establish their individual independent republics. In January 1920 the Western powers gave *de facto* recognition to the Transcaucasian republics. The Red Army, however, seized control in the region that spring. By 1921 the Bolsheviks gained complete control of Transcaucasia and established the Soviet Transcaucasian Republic. In 1936, Armenia, Azerbaijan and Georgia became republics of the Soviet Union.

Ethnicity

In Central Asia, the search for national identity has taken place against a complex demographic and cultural background. Before the nineteenth century the ties of the various peoples of the region reached far beyond the modern-day boundaries of Central Asia to the Ottoman Empire, Persia, and China. This history has left an imprint on all the new states. Ethnically, most of the

8

peoples of the region are Turkic. Their languages link them with Turkey.

On the other hand, at one time or another, many of the region's peoples have also sustained cultural and economic links with Iran. This is especially true of the Tajiks. They speak a variant of the Persian language and share many traditions. Despite many common characteristics, relations between Tajiks and the Turkic peoples of Central Asia have been distinguished by a chronic element of cultural and political competition.

During the 1930s, Stalin's imposition of a draconian policy of cultural segregation put an end to the considerable cross-border relations between Central Asian republics and their southern neighbours. As a result of change of the alphabets of the Central Asian languages to the Latin in the 1920s, the literature and publications of many neighbouring countries were made unintelligible to new generations of Central Asia. The renunciation of the Arabic script corroded Central Asia's weakening ties with Persia and reduced its cultural and religious interaction with the Arab world. After 1928 the introduction of Cyrillic and the abandonment of the new Latin alphabet used by Tajiks and some Turkic groups undercut the region's ties with Turkey.

At the start of the Soviet period none of the Central Asian peoples had a clearly developed sense of national identity. For the majority of the population supranational identities, particularly an association with Islam, had been more important. During the Soviet period distinctive Central Asian national identities gradually combined around the national republics. Still nationalist incentives in the region remained relatively weak at the time of the Soviet collapse. National consciousness has developed in the cities of Central Asia. However, the identity of rural inhabitants still is defined primarily in terms of religious or regional affiliation.

None of the countries of Central Asia is ethnically homogeneous. The ethnic cleavage divides ethnic Russians from ethnic Central Asians. All the new states of the region have sizeable Russian minorities. Approximately eight to ten per cent of the population of Tajikistan, Uzbekistan and Turkmenistan, 22 per cent in Kyrgyzstan, and nearly 38 per cent in Kazakhstan are ethnic Russians. The majority of these Russians are not recent immigrants from Russia. Most of them have come to Central Asia in waves of immigration, either in the late Tsarist period, in the 1920s and 1930s, or during the Virgin Lands period under Khrushchev. Most of these Russian residents are second or third generation immigrants, who were born in the Central Asian countries. Many local Russians probably regard their country of residence as their home.

The relationship between local Russians and ethnic Central Asians is critical to the future of Central Asian states. It is important because it affects Russia's political relations with the new states. It is important also because in most cases the economic and technical skills furnished by the local Russians cannot be replaced in the short term by indigenous Central Asian manpower. Russians make up the bulk of the managerial and technical personnel in mining, energy production, and other key industrial sectors.

There can be found a number of anxieties and hostilities in the relations between ethnic Central Asians and local Russians. The first outcome of this historical baggage is a rise in anti-Russian feelings among ethnic Central Asians. For their part, many local Russians fear that they may become the target of ethnic violence. Since 1989 all the Central Asian governments have adopted new language laws that impinge on the privileged social and political position of local Russians. The appearance in most of the Central Asian states of political parties and organisations based on anti-Russian feelings is a natural consequence of these circumstances. Consequently the number of Russians leaving Central Asia has increased sharply since 1989.

Another important element in the volatile ethnic mix of the Central Asian states is the presence of large ethnic Central Asian minorities in several countries of the region. In Tajikistan Uzbeks constitute nearly a quarter of the total population. In Kyrgyzstan

Uzbeks account for almost 13 per cent of the population. More than 20 per cent of all Tajiks live in Uzbekistan, and seven per cent of all Uzbeks live in Tajikistan. These internal ethnic divisions have major implications for the future of the region. Long-standing tensions between Uzbeks and Tajiks in the Fergana Valley constitutes probably the most explosive issue for the region.

The states of the Caucasus stand out as a group for their relatively high level of homogeneity. Georgia is the least homogeneous of the three Transcaucasian republics where only 70 per cent of the population consist of ethnic Georgians. Georgia and Armenia have long maintained a dynamic indigenous cultural life based on written languages that are centuries older than the Russian language. Armenia is the most homogenous with a strong national identity and a politically experienced élite.

However, regional warfare has devastated the Caucasus. In Georgia, the dissolution of Soviet power has ventilated hostilities between ethnic Georgians and Abkhazians and Ossetians. The South Ossetians have attempted to unite with the North Ossetians, who occupy territory across the border in Russia. South Ossetians' guerrilla warfare against Georgian authorities and efforts under the vigorous nationalist Zviad Gamsakhurdia to suppress the separatist movement led to thousands of casualties and tens of thousands of refugees.

The conflict over Abkhazia appears similarly intractable. Abkhazians seek complete independence from Georgia and the establishment of their own state. But ethnic Abkhazians now make up only 18 per cent of the approximately 537,000 people living in the Georgian controlled Abkhazia, compared with almost 46 per cent Georgians. The Tbilisi government has not been inclined to compromise. The results were government repression and violent communal conflicts. In 1992 Georgia fell into the grip of ethnic and civil war, violence and instability replacing law and order.

The relations between Armenia and Azerbaijan have become an even more serious source of conflict for the region. What began in

1988 as a political controversy between two countries over the control of Azerbaijani-held enclave Nagorno-Karabakh, population of which is predominantly Armenian, has been escalated into an exhausting war. This war between Azerbaijan and Armenia has become the clearest illustration in the post-Soviet states of the destructive potential of nationalism.

Throughout the Soviet period, Armenia chaffed at the arbitrary administrative transfer of the predominantly Armenian area of Nagorno-Karabakh to Azerbaijan made by Stalin. In 1921, he thus laid the foundations for today's Armenian-Azeri dispute by creating the Nagorno-Karabakh autonomous region out of a mountainous portion of eastern Armenia and placing it under Azeri control. In 1988, emboldened by perestroika and Gorbachev's indecisiveness, Armenians began agitating for the return of the enclave. Following the demise of the Soviet system, communal violence and escalating national passions created a long war of attrition. Azerbaijani setbacks at the hands of the Armenian forces on the battlefield helped to undermine the position of Azerbaijan's first democratically elected president, Abulfaz Elchibey.

In all likelihood the search for national identity in the new states of the Caucasus and Central Asia will take decades to reach clear outcomes. Even at its best, the creation of a national identity is fraught with difficulty. There is a serious risk that some of the attempts of the national leaders to divide the population along ethnic lines on a permanent basis might trigger a spiral of domestic conflict.

The Impact of Religion

In the post-Soviet era the new states of the Caucasus and Central Asia are experiencing a religious revival. According to many observers the failure of the Communist vision has created a moral vacuum that religion seems suited to fill. In a period marked by uncertain political values and shaky institutions, religion is likely to have a magnified political effect. However, the extent to which religion will strengthen or weaken the political cohesion of the new states is by no means clear at this stage; and there exists a substantial body of opinion that emphasises the very different role played by Islam in Central Asia and doubts its longer term political significance.

Islam is the dominant religion of Central Asia's fifty million inhabitants. Most Central Asian Muslims adhere to the Sunni form of Islam. In the pre-Soviet period, Islam constituted an important element in the identity of the Central Asian peoples. However, it did not generate a set of political loyalties that overrode all others. Islam constituted one of several markers of identity, with tribal and clan loyalties and attachments to subnational regions.

Like other religious confessions, Islam was subjected to devastating attacks during the early Soviet era, especially under Stalin. In the late 1950s, Khrushchev undertook a militant new anti-religious assault, waging a renewed fierce campaign against Islamic beliefs and customs. Despite all the anti-Islamic campaigns a strong attachment to Islam has survived among the inhabitants of the Central Asia. It is partly related to the fact that by comparison with many other religions existing in the region, Islamic beliefs and practices have been woven more deeply into the texture of everyday life. It is also partly due to the ability of Islam to create an anti-establishment self-identity. The demise of centrally-sponsored atheism has cleared the way for the growth of religious observances. New mosques have been constructed and more young people have entered into religious education. These developments raise concern of the possibility of an Islamic revival affecting the evolution of the Central Asian states.

In this aspect, Tajikistan occupies a special place among the newly independent states. Tajikistan lacks the economic significance of Turkmenistan and Kazakhstan as it lacks also Uzbekistan's political weight. However, due to a unique combination of culture and ideology its relations with militant Islam carry a special role. Of all the new Muslim states, Tajikistan is the only Farsi-speaking state with a strong linkage with Iran. It clearly has been the most politicised with active Islamic tendencies among Central Asian states. Tajikistan's Islamic movement started in the mid-1970s and particularly grew under the impact of the Soviet invasion of Afghanistan.

Overall, the Islamic factor has affected the relations among the Central Asian states in a fundamental way. The fight against the 'Islamic fundamentalism' brought together a variety of domestic, regional, and international actors. The concern over the Islamic threat has been shared by all the Central Asian political leaders. The containment of the Islamic threat has also been carried out by Russia. Countering the Islamic threat in general has become a central defining element in Russian foreign policy toward the entire former Soviet south.

In the Caucasus religion has played an important but variable political role. In the lands of Armenia and Georgia Christianity took root long before the acceptance of Christianity by Kievan Rus. In Azerbaijan Islam has historically been the dominant religion. Unlike the Muslims of Central Asia, who are predominantly Sunnis, most Azeris belong to the Shiite branch of Islam like the Iranians. Though Azerbaijan is predominantly secular and does not own a tradition of fundamental Islam, during the recent years more militant Islamic movement has been reported to be gaining strength.

Islamic-Christian religious differences have contributed to the tensions in the region. Particularly in the armed conflict between Muslim Azerbaijanis and Christian Armenians distinct religious identities antagonised the positions and perceptions of each side.

14

3   The Economy

Regional Economic Development

Most of the countries of Central Asia face a difficult economic future. In the Soviet period, Moscow's policy towards the region called for the Central Asian states to specialise in a few primary sectors. This policy has imposed a high price on the region in both economic and environmental terms. With Central Asia's population growth one of the highest in the world, there is a premium on job creation, and resource maximisation. The Central Asian states are among the poorest of the former Soviet Union in per capita terms. In addition, the problems caused by ploughing up large expanses of *steppe* lands in Kazakhstan during the Khrushchev period led to a degradation of the land in such a short time that much of the acreage had to be removed from grain production altogether, and chemical fertilisers have been used in doses so vast that water and land have become contaminated.

Central Asia has a high economic dependency on Russia. Most of Central Asia's trade is still with the Russian Federation. The close economic ties with Russia are reflected in the fact that most Central Asian leaders have opted to remain within the Rouble Zone. Kazakhstan in particular has continued to press integration with Russia. It seems that the Central Asians will be dependent on the Russian market, monetary system and financial expertise for the indefinite future.

However, there are certain elements in the current economic situation that allow for a more optimistic long-term economic forecast. These countries have rich mineral and energy resources. None of the Central Asian states, with the exception of Uzbekistan, is dependent on Russian gas and crude oil. Turkmenistan and Kazakhstan have large deposits of oil and gas. These resources have the potential to become the driving force behind a broad-based economic development.

Since the demise of the Soviet Union, the Central Asian states have made some progress in 'marketising' and privatising their economies. The Kazakh government has initiated a programme of privatisation that would redistribute ownership of retail establishments, dwellings, and some industry. In May 1992 the Nazarbayev government signed a joint venture agreement with the US oil company *Chevron* to develop the *Tengiz* oil field.

Kyrgyzstan, one of the poorest nations of the region, has large reserves of mercury, antimony and uranium, and has so far been energetic in attempting to attract foreign investment. Trade regulations have been modified and tax and custom barriers simplified. Kyrgyzstan also has introduced new rules to encourage and secure foreign capital.

Turkmenistan, the southernmost Central Asian republic, has the greatest natural gas and oil reserves. Although it lacks a solid industrial base, given the nation's rich resources and small population, it is in a better economic position than most of its Central Asian neighbours. Turkmenistan has already established commercial relations with Japan, China and European countries, and is becoming more active in external relations.

Uzbekistan is the world's third largest producer of cotton and the major source of the crop for the former Soviet Union. Industry is largely undeveloped, but Uzbekistan does account for a third of the gold mined in the former Soviet Union. There is also a strong potential for developing trade. In all parts of Central Asia, Uzbeks are regarded as the most skilful traders.

Tajikistan is the poorest and most underdeveloped of the former Soviet republics. There are, however, rich coal and oil deposits, and the republic has been a major producer of uranium.

The Caucasian states of Georgia, Armenia, and Azerbaijan were devastated by the chaos unleashed by the Soviet break-up. The disruption of traditional trading links with Russia and the other former Soviet republics crippled their economies and devastated the livelihood of the local population. Furthermore, the war of attrition in each of the states has turned economic hardship into actual collapse. The socio-economic burden of war has devastated the economies of the three countries. Their leaders have found their policy capabilities and options far more limited than they would otherwise have been prepared to accept.

The bitter war with Azerbaijan over Nagorno-Karabakh has proved disastrous for Armenia. The human and economic costs of the conflict have been heightened by Armenia's landlocked location. The closure by Azerbaijan of a pipeline supplying 80 per cent of Armenia's gas has created extreme hardship in Erevan. Since 1991 Azerbaijan has maintained a rail and road blockade against Armenia. The ongoing ethnic conflict with Azerbaijan and the Azeri blockade overshadows the government's commitment to economic reform.

Georgia is now effectively a 'de-industrialised' nation. About 90 per cent of Georgia's industrial plants are standing idle. The circumstances under which Georgia was to attempt a transformation were by far the worst in the entire area formerly occupied by the USSR. The Georgian economy has been shattered by secessionist conflicts in Abkhazia and South Ossetia. Conflict has blocked the influx of foreign aid and investment that Georgian leaders expected after the accession of former Soviet foreign minister Eduard Shevardnadze to power in March 1992. Georgia's economic progress has therefore been severely obstructed by its political instability.

Azerbaijan appears not to face as troubling an economic future as either Armenia or Georgia. Economic factors, however, will likely continue to influence its policies. It is difficult to say that Azerbaijan has made progress with market economic reforms. It remains, in effect, a centrally planned economy with no market or independent financial structures. Azerbaijan has sought to increase its economic links with the Turkic world for political and military, as well as economic, reasons.

Despite these problems all three Transcaucasian states have rich potential in terms of resources and material. Georgian agriculture is, by Soviet standards, a success. Large quantities of citrus fruit, tea and vegetables are produced. Food processing industries are well-developed. Many large and turbulent rivers give Georgia a great capacity for hydroelectric development. Armenia's industrial infrastructure is reasonably well developed and it has received financial and moral support from the three million Armenians abroad. Azerbaijan, the largest of the three states of the Transcaucasus, has extensive oil and gas fields. In an effort to earn the maximum amount of hard currency from energy exports, the government is actively inviting international energy companies to attract investment.

Given Central Asia's and Transcaucasia's great economic potential there is reason to be optimistic. The territory contains more natural wealth than is found anywhere else on the planet. If fully developed with modern technology, Central Asia's and Transcaucasia's vast supplies of oil and other natural resources could create growth unprecedented in the region. International assistance and privatisation could stimulate business activity. However, the vast distances and harsh environmental conditions, combined with a poorly developed infrastructure, make extraction and transportation of these resources difficult and costly. Large-scale energy, mining, and infrastructure projects pose a serious limitation. Major projects of this sort will require a long time to be completed. In the short-term, they will have no significant positive effect on the standard of living in Central Asia and Transcaucasia.

Turkey's Economic Relations With the Region

Following the end of the Cold War and the disintegration of the Soviet Union, Turkey launched several initiatives for increased economic co-operation and shared prosperity in Eurasia. One of these initiatives was to constitute the 'Black Sea Economic Co-operation Zone' for multilateral dialogue and co-operation. The other initiative was the enlargement of the 'Economic Co-operation Organisation' (ECO) through the participation of the newly independent states of Central Asia and Azerbaijan as well as Afghanistan.

Turkey's economic relations with the states of Central Asia and the Caucasus range from planning the establishment of special banks to regulate financial relations to setting up barter companies. Creating a transportation and communications system as well as small and medium-sized private enterprises to solve problems pertaining to basic utilities has become a short-term goal.[3]

Setting up the financial framework for developed trade has been given priority by the Turkish government, and a special bank for this purpose was established in Turkey. The *Eximbank* explores the possibilities of aid to the Turkic republics. In addition, a Turkish Central Asian Bank has opened branches in the region.

Teletas, a leading Turkish telecommunications company, has signed an agreement with Uzbekistan to develop communications technology. Furthermore, the Turkish government was asked to represent Uzbekistan's interests abroad, particularly with respect to the production and transportation of agricultural produce, building of light industrial complexes, the search for and extraction of minerals, construction infrastructure for tourism, cooperation in transport, and operating food industries.

A Turkish construction company, *BMB*, and its local counterpart, have agreed on the construction of a natural gas pipeline in Turkmenistan. Its annual flow capacity will eventually reach 15 to 20 billion cubic meters. Another Turkish firm, Konkur Insaat, is going to build a large tourist complex and a cultural centre in Turkmenistan.

Turkey has established a joint consultation mechanism with Kazakhstan. The two sides have agreed to establish and improve waterways, rail and air links to facilitate trade. Teletas has began manufacturing electronics and other modern communications equipment in Kazakhstan.

---

[3] T. Ataöv, 'Turkey, CIS and Eastern Europe', *Turkey and Europe*, ed. by C. Balkir and A. M. Williams, London and New York, 1993, p. 201.

Trade agreements with Kyrgyzstan cover almost every field including agriculture, industry, mining, construction, tourism, health, communications and transport.

Today, business school teachers from Istanbul commute regularly to Baku, and Azeri students study business and management in Turkey. Economic relations between the two countries are, however, not as developed as had been expected. In spite of the linguistic, cultural affinity as well as the market potential, Turkey's trade relations with Azerbaijan do not rank at the top among Azeri trading partners: Turkey comes fourth in terms of volume of trade after Russian Federation, Turkmenistan, Ukraine and Iran.

Georgia is considered a gateway for Turkey to the Caucasian, Russian and Central Asian markets. Although the Georgian economy is in bad shape, the cross-border barter trade is flourishing and some Turkish entrepreneurs are investing in the fields of small and medium size manufacturing, food packing and metallurgical industries. The shortage of energy and political uncertainties are the main obstacles for further investment in the country.

Although there is no formal trade agreement between Turkey and Armenia, cross-border barter trade started immediately after the collapse of the Soviet Union. The twice-weekly train running between Kars and Gümrü (former Leninakan) had not only been transporting goods but was packed with mostly Armenian passengers who had been purchasing various Turkish products ranging from electrical appliances, canned food, beverages, detergents to textile products in exchange for vodka, brandy, livestock and hide. Following the increasing level of fighting between Azeris and Armenians in early 1993, Turkey halted all border crossings and transhipment of goods to Armenia. However, the potential for more trade between Turkey and Armenia still exists.

Naturally, Turkey is not the only country interested in the region. While Turkey has been building up its relationship with the

Central Asian and the Caucasian Turkic people, they have shown an equal interest in cultivating ties with other interested countries.

Iran and four former Soviet republics, Azerbaijan, Kazakhstan, Russia and Turkmenistan, formed the 'Caspian Sea Cooperation Council' (CSCC) in 1992. The CSCC appeared to be Iran's response to the Turkish-sponsored Black Sea Economic Cooperation scheme. Trade between Azerbaijan and Iran has expanded in recent years and has not been affected by the changes of leadership in Baku. Iran agreed with Azerbaijan to cooperate in oil production and also with Kazakhstan on transportation of goods between the Caspian Sea ports of the two littoral states. The Nakhicevan enclave of Azerbaijan and the eastern Azerbaijan region of Iran signed an economic and cultural agreement to set up a common market at the Jolfa border gate.

In addition to Turkey and Iran, a relative newcomer to the region has now become a significant player. The United States, and to a lesser extent, its western allies have been most prominently visible in the realm of economics, particularly in fuel extraction. Since the dissolution of the Soviet Union, the United States has shown great interest in helping to exploit the oil resources of the Caucasus and Central Asia. Five American companies form the backbone of an international consortium that signed a major deal with the Azerbaijani government for the extraction of oil from three major off-shore fields in September 1994.

Despite increasing relations with the other powers, particularly Turkey and Iran, today the most important factor in the economic development of the new states is the critical importance of their relations with Russia. This has made their relations with each other of secondary importance. For the Central Asians and the Caucasians Russia remains the main force to be reckoned with. Most of the new republics' trade is still with the Russian Federation. The five newly independent states of Central Asia are still dependent upon Russia for transport facilities to export their primary commodities. Military ties remain close. Their political and economic interdependence, together with Russia's determination not to relinquish control over this vast area, means that relations with no other country can command greater priority for Central Asian and Transcaucasian states.

The general advantage in the current competition between Turkey, Iran and Russia rests with Russia. Today it is clear that deep residual economic and military interdependence connects the newly independent states to Russia. The weight of its past political, military, economic and cultural rule is everywhere in evidence, and it could take a long time for the Turkic countries to surmount these vestiges of colonialism.

4 Russia and Turkey: Old Rivals, New Relationship

History

Russia and Turkey, brought together by geography and separated by ideology and regime interests, have had a long history of both conflict and cooperation. Russian-Turkish relations inherited a long tradition of rivalry in the lands of the Ottoman Empire which went back over centuries. Traditionally Russia endeavoured to achieve two goals on its southern flank: to prevent any hostile attack from the rear through the Black Sea and to keep open its only exit to warm waters.

Ottoman control over the Black Sea had been decisively established in the fifteenth century. With their capture of Constantinople in 1453, the Ottoman Turks became the sovereigns of the Straits. The capture of the Crimea in 1475 brought the whole coastline of the Black Sea under the total control of the Ottoman Empire. Following this victory, the Sultan asserted what became known as 'the ancient rule of the Ottoman Empire'. According to it the *Sublime Porte* denied entrance into the Black Sea to the ships of all foreign nations. For three centuries, with the exception of certain commercial privileges given to the Venetians for a short period, the Black Sea remained closed to all ships except those of the Ottoman Empire.

A change came when Russia captured Azov in 1696 and endeavoured to gain a share in the Black Sea coastline. This was the result of the Treaty of Küçük Kaynarca which was signed in 1774 between the Russian and Ottoman Empires. The treaty came after a war in which a Russian fleet had entered the Mediterranean and threatened the coasts of Anatolia. By the treaty the Ottoman Empire ceded to Russia the Kuban and Terek areas in the Black Sea *steppe* which had hitherto been under Turkish suzerainty. The Ottoman Turks also surrendered the port of Azov at the mouth of the Don, together with the fortresses of Kerch and Yenikale which controlled the straits joining the Sea of Azov and the Black Sea proper. More importantly, Russia acquired a relatively small area between the lower courses of the rivers Bug and Dnieper, together with the mouth of the latter. It thus gained for the first time a foothold, though as yet a limited one, on the Black Sea. In addition to these territorial gains, the treaty of Küçük Kaynarca opened the Black Sea and the Straits for Russian commercial vessels. Thereafter, 'the ancient rule of the Straits' could no longer be enforced by the Ottoman rulers.

The Treaty of Hünkar Iskelesi signed between Russia and the Ottoman Empire in 1833 represented the farthest advance ever made by Russia towards solving the problem of the Straits in its own favour to the exclusion of other influences. This treaty opened the Straits to Russian warships. According to a secret article of this agreement, the Ottoman government agreed to close the Straits of the Dardanelles in case of war to any foreign warship. This secret article provided complete security for Russia in the case of war by allowing the passage of the Russian warships as it was given the status of an ally.

With the Bolsheviks' seizure of power in Petrograd in November 1917 and as a result of the specific historical circumstances related to the end of the First World War, Turkish-Russian relations underwent a radical change. Following the defeat of the Ottoman Empire in the war, large parts of the country were occupied by the Allied forces. The Sultan's government in the Ottoman capital conceded complete surrender, but there were nationalistic stirrings throughout the country. When Greek forces landed in Anatolia in May 1919, Mustafa Kemal raised the banner of an independent post-Ottoman struggle in the non-occupied parts of central and eastern Anatolia.

In this war of liberation Soviet Russia was the first and principal ally of Kemalist Turkey. In March 1921, a treaty of friendship was concluded between the two nations. Soviet-Turkish relations during the 1920s continued to be closer than those between Moscow and any other non-communist country.

Nonetheless, geography has predisposed Russia and Turkey to a history of conflict. Their cooperation was never free from suspicion. The founder of the Turkish Republic, Mustafa Kemal, understood the value of ties with the newly emergent Soviet regime in Moscow. He regarded the relationship important for protecting his rear and as a source of financial and material support in the conflict with the Western powers.

Mustafa Kemal's determination to revise the Lausanne Treaty and to eliminate restrictions on Turkish sovereignty over the Black Sea Straits contributed to the erosion of trust between the two countries. After the Montreux Conference on the future of the Dardanelles in 1936, there was a certain cooling off in the friendship. The close relationship between Moscow and the Kemalist regime in Ankara came to an end in 1939. The secret Ribbentrop-Molotov Accord to divide eastern Europe in 1940 gave the Soviets a free hand in the Straits, which changed Moscow's interests in the Near East overnight. After the Second World War, friction between Turkey and the Soviet Union increased. When the Soviets championed the Kurdish republic of Mahabad in 1945–46, alarm bells rang in Ankara. In 1945, the Soviet government demanded both the return of Kars and Ardahan provinces and a base on the Straits area.

Turkey's entry into NATO in 1952 provided reassurance against the Soviet threat. The Alliance used Turkish territory as an 'unsinkable aircraft carrier'. This raised Turkey's strategic profile, but greatly increased concerns in Moscow about a possible NATO attack through Turkish lands. Following the death of Stalin in

1953, however, relations gradually improved. The new leadership in Moscow showed a clear intention to maintain normalised relations with Turkey. The removal of the Jupiter missiles, following the Cuban missile crisis in 1962, reduced Turkey's strategic value at a stroke. In this new era of détente, a measure of cooperation between Ankara and Moscow became possible. In the 1970s, Moscow provided Turkey with several hundred million dollars' worth of economic projects.

Nevertheless, all these were not enough to eliminate the mark of suspicion from the essence of Soviet-Turkish relations. The Soviets continued to criticise the presence of American military facilities in Turkey, opposed Turkey's intervention in Cyprus in 1974, while Turkey denounced the Soviet invasion of Afghanistan in December 1979.

The advent of Gorbachev brought a visible change in the political environment for the Soviet-Turkish relations. This led Turgut Özal, then Turkish Prime Minister, to travel to the Soviet Union in 1986. In conjunction with Özal's visit, Moscow agreed to open a new land crossing point with Turkey at Sarp on the Black Sea border.

As *perestroika* and *glasnost* picked up in intensity, several other obstacles were removed. In June 1989, *Bizim Radyo* [Our Radio], the clandestine Turkish Communist Party organ, ended 31 years of radio broadcasts from Eastern Germany. Ankara took this as a Soviet gesture of friendship. Also important in promoting greater confidence was the Soviet withdrawal from Afghanistan. This period also saw exchanges of naval visits, which was considered further evidence of a gradual relaxation of military tension. In March 1991, just before his fatal stroke, Turgut Özal, then the President of the Republic, travelled to Russia for the second time in five years. This time he visited two important republics, Kazakhstan and Azerbaijan. As a result of this trip, Russia agreed to allow Turkey to reopen its consulate general in Baku, after half a century.

The collapse of the Soviet Union and the emergence of the independent states along the southern frontier of the Russian Federation eliminated the common border separating the Russian/Soviet state from its long-term historical antagonist, Turkey. The Soviet collapse established a huge buffer zone in Central Asia and Transcaucasia between the Russian Federation and Turkey. The demise of the Soviet Union also transformed this buffer zone into an area of competition between these immediate outsiders. A greatly altered environment has reawakened some old problems and necessitated reassessment of long-held assumptions about the Russo-Turkish relations in the area.

As the transition accelerated and the Soviet Union was succeeded by the Commonwealth of Independent States in late 1991, Ankara focused its attention more and more on the Turkic republics of the former Soviet Union. By the end of 1991, Turkey had formally recognised all republics and established diplomatic relations. However, conscious of Russia's military might, the Ankara leadership sought to avoid hostility and controversy with its northern neighbour.

Russia's 'Near Abroad' Policy

After the collapse of the Soviet Union, Russia lost interest in the former Soviet republics for a short period of time. This was simply due to the euphoria over the newly found independence and the end of the old system. The Russian leadership was preoccupied during this short transitional period with the need to institutionalise its own independence. It was also true that Russia's diplomatic efforts in this phase were more concentrated on developing close relations with the United States and the West. For these reasons, Russia did not initially express interest in the newly independent states of the former Soviet Union.

Russia's initial indifference to defining the character of its relations with the Caucasus and Central Asian states was changed by the homeward flow of refugees from these countries. Hundreds of thousands of second and third generation ethnic Russians began to flood Russia with their stories of anti-Russian campaigns and sentiments that had forced them to flee. These generated public sentiment against some of non-Russian newly independent states.

Gradually, such emotions reached such a high level that the Russian leadership could no longer ignore the issue. This was the beginning of what has been termed as the 'Russian Near Abroad policy'. The Near Abroad policy proclaims the newly independent states a zone of Russia's vital interests. It emphasises Russia's special external responsibility for the protection of newly independent states' borders. It also means protection of rights and interests of almost ten million Russians living in the newly independent non-Russian republics.

Military ties between Moscow and the newly independent republics remain close. Treaties of friendship and cooperation between Russia and the republics serve as the legal and institutional basis for close cooperation in the area of defence. Russian military officers who have spent their lives in these republics have a vested interest in drawing Moscow's attention to the Near Abroad.

Presently Russia maintains a keen interest in the events of the Caucasus and Central Asia. Russia has understandable security concerns in these regions. Moscow fears that regional instability may threaten the southern Russian provinces. This explains Russia's peacekeeping role in Georgia and Moscow's efforts to mediate a peaceful solution over Nagorno-Karabakh. Russia is determined to have a military presence in the Caucasus. In Russian decision-making circles a consensus has now emerged that recognises the increasing importance of maintaining close relations with the former Soviet republics.

Constraints in Russian-Turkish Relations

During the last few years, consequential and significant differences of opinion have emerged in the relations between Russia and Turkey. Although none is likely to jeopardise their business-like reconciliation, each perceptual and policy difference has the potential to turn into an issue. These differences are reminders to the two countries of how much work is required to resolve the points of concern.

Russia is not prepared to allow Turkey to acquire enhanced influence in the Caucasus and Central Asia at Moscow's expense. Deep-rooted fears of pan-Turkism were kindled with the accession to power in Azerbaijan of Elçibey. To many Russians Islam is closely associated with fundamentalism and the Muslim threat from the south.

Probably, the first important test for the new relationship had been the explosive conflict between Azerbaijan and Armenia. By early 1992, Armenian forces had completed the conquest of Azeri strongholds in Nagorno-Karabakh. This was followed by further Armenian attacks, this time on the Azerbaijani enclave of Nakhicevan. All this development brought Turkey into the conflict with the possibility of a major confrontation with Russia. When Ankara condemned Armenian aggression with vague references to possible military action, this was regarded an intervention from a NATO power in Russia.

The disintegration of Yugoslavia also caused a build-up of tension in Turco-Russian relations. Serbian attacks against the Muslims in Bosnia increased suspicions in Turkey that religious considerations governed European attitudes toward Muslims. Ankara campaigned hard for Turkish forces to be included in all military and peacekeeping operations. Russia, on the other hand, appeared sympathetic to the Serbs. In early 1994, Russia dispatched its own forces to take part in the peacekeeping operations. That was widely regarded as favourable to the Serbs. The Russian move gave the Turks an argument to overcome the reserve with which Turkish forces had previously been regarded by the international community. In June 1994, Turkish ground forces were allowed to join the peacekeeping process.

The historical controversy over the use of the Black Sea Straits increasingly became an issue and, the Turkish-Russian differences have become more pronounced. Congestion in this waterway led the Turkish authorities to consider additional regulations for piloting ships in its narrow confines. Russia objected to the idea of such restrictions. Russian interest in using Novorrossisk as an oil transhipment point for tankers through the Straits caused further concern in Turkey. Such a step has been regarded an unacceptable level of hazard to Istanbul, particularly along the narrow and winding waterway between the two shores of the Bosphorus.

Russian policy toward the Kurdish issue constitutes another significant difference of opinion. In the spring of 1994, a conference of the Kurdistan Workers' Party (PKK) was publicly convened in Moscow. Some commentators saw the conference as a move to retaliate against Turkish involvement with the Chechens. In late October 1994, a confederation of CIS Kurdish Organisations was created in Moscow.

On the economic front, there is the issue of the Caspian oil, particularly the extraction of the off-shore oil and its transportation to West European markets. In 1993, Elçibey signed a far-reaching agreement with a Western consortium, headed by British Petroleum. According to this agreement, when extracted, the Caspian oil was to be transported to Turkey's Mediterranean coast via Georgia. This agreement was not acceptable to Moscow. Significantly, one of Aliyev's first official acts as the president of Azerbaijan was to inform the consortium that the original contract would have to be renegotiated. In February 1994, Azerbaijan and Great Britain signed a memorandum providing for cooperation in the exploitation of some of the Caspian oil fields. Russian Ministry of Foreign Affairs protested by saying that Baku had no right to dispose of the petroleum deposits because there is "no sectoral demarcation of the seabed in the Caspian Sea".[4]

On 20 September 1994, Socar, the Azeri state oil company, signed an agreement with an international consortium, which consisted

---

[4] *Izvestiia*, 7 June 1994.

of five US companies, British Petroleum, Statoil (Norway), as well as the Turkish and Saudi national oil companies. According to the terms, Azerbaijan would receive approximately 80 per cent of the profits.

Moscow and Ankara differed on the location of the pipeline that would transport the Azeri petroleum to its West European destinations. With more than 15 billion barrels of oil located below the surface of the Caucasus, Central Asia and the Caspian Sea, the producers, Azerbaijan, Kazakhstan and the others consider their fuel resources as a means of escaping both relative poverty and Russian domination. Turkey, Iran and Russia have been vitally interested in having the pipelines from the region constructed in their respective territories.

Areas of Convergence

Despite their differences, for the time being common concerns transcend the competitive ambitions of Moscow and Ankara. As long as both governments remain committed to their present priorities in Central Asia and Transcaucasia, their relationship is solidly grounded in mutual interests.

The end of the Cold War opened the way for new areas of cooperation. The Black Sea Economic Cooperation project initiated by Ankara offered an avenue for cooperation. Originally conceived in 1990, this initiative has sought to encourage economic links among the Black Sea states.

During the international crisis with respect to Saddam Hussein's invasion of Kuwait, both Russia and Turkey felt the need to be part of the general international consensus. Later each had its own particular reasons to ask for the economic sanctions on Iraq to be lifted. Turkey felt the impact of losing the lucrative oil transit fees from the pipeline through Turkey from the northern Iraqi fields. Russia hoped that permitting Iraqi oil sales would provide Baghdad with foreign exchange to repay extensive debts to Russia for military equipment supplied in an earlier era.

Russia and Turkey have strong vested interests in keeping their differences under control. It is clear that Russia will not be willing to abandon its sphere of influence in the Caucasus and Central Asia. Ethnic conflict in the region offers Russia extensive opportunities to regain influence.

Turkish policy toward the CIS is based on a feeling of identity with the Turkic republics and a desire to make sure that Moscow does not gain undue influence over them. These considerations might push Turkey to reinforce cultural and educational links and increasing economic deals with these newly independent states. Turkish business interests, particularly oil, occupy a central place in this strategy. Efforts to promote pipelines from Central Asia and Azerbaijan will continue to clash with Russian interests in controlling oil production and transportation.

The Turkish-Russian relationship, complex and increasingly wide-ranging, is driven by necessity and pragmatism, devoid of illusions or the influence of natural affinities. Cooperation is prompted by calculations of mutual economic advantage, by an interest in stability on their borders. These convergent aims, noticeable particularly during the early decades of the Turkish Republic, but then overshadowed by the Cold War, have taken on new significance in the post-Soviet era.

Turkey and Russia have a vested interest in seeing that regional political instability does not disrupt their bilateral cooperation. Since the two countries no longer share a common border, the flow of their trade depends on the cooperation of the republics in between.

Moscow and Ankara recognise that for trade to flourish, there must be stability in the region between them. In the Caucasus, the two countries are working to negotiate a settlement between Armenia and Azerbaijan. Whatever agreement they can reach will probably leave Moscow in a stronger position. But as long as Russia's military presence is kept limited, Turkey might be satisfied with the outcome. Russia has maintained close military relations with Tajikistan, Uzbekistan, Turkmenistan and Kyrgyzstan. This was mainly because of requests from the pro-Moscow leaders of these republics. All the treaties that Russia signed with the four Muslim Central Asian republics reaffirm the inviolability of existing borders. This is somewhat reassuring to Turkey.

5 Conclusions

In the period immediately after the collapse of the Soviet Union, Turkey had great expectations about establishing major influence in many parts of Central Asia and the Caucasus. It was claimed that there existed a very special relationship between Turkey, the Caucasus and Central Asian republics. This was based on the belief that ethnic, linguistic, religious, and cultural affinities would pave the way for close ties and a major presence. In this, Ankara naively underestimated the functional and operational ties that continued to bind the newly independent states to Moscow. Turkey exulted too soon and assumed too much by thinking that the establishment of a TV station beaming broadcasts to Central Asia would result in immediate outpourings of pro-Turkish sentiments in the region. It was equally a mistake to think that the Turks would be welcome to play the role of a new big brother to the region's Turkic-speaking peoples.

If Turkey thought it could lead the new states of Central Asia and the Caucasus into a new world, it soon found out that its capacities did not suffice to undertake this momentous project. Turkey's economic limitations, especially in view of a significant Russian role in the economic survival of the new republics, is an important modifier of its influence.

The situation was exacerbated by the fact that Turkey promised more than it could deliver. As a result Turks have learned that limited capabilities mean limited influence. It has been realised that influence building is a more costly and complex process than had been originally expected. Today it has been realised that Turkey cannot cope with all the challenges and also exploit all emerging opportunities at the same time.

Now that the initial euphoria has waned, it has become apparent that Turkey's relations with this part of the world are not necessarily or automatically going to be as strong as once proclaimed. Today, after many shifts, it is very likely that Turkey's relations with the Caucasus and Central Asia will settle on a more realistic level. Clearly, a strong relationship is developing. However, it has to be seen in a wider context.

Turkey has made a genuine and continuing commitment to the Central Asian and Caucasian countries. Turkish businessmen have invested heavily in the region. Political and military agreements are being signed between government leaders. For the first time in Turkey's history, an official institute has been established to regulate the relations with Central Asia and the Caucasus: TIKA (Türk Isbirligi ve Kalkinma Ajansi), the Turkish acronym for the Turkish International Cooperation Agency (which in English is rendered as TICA). A Minister of State in charge of economy in the Cabinet is entrusted with an overall brief to supervise and co-ordinate the relationships between Turkey and the region.

Today we are witnessing a return to a multipolar competition for advantage in Transcaucasia and Central Asia, reminiscent of that which took place in the seventeenth and eighteenth centuries. In addition to Turkey, Russia and Iran constitute the immediate strategic triad. However, unlike their past rivalry, that of today is cooperative as well as competitive. They all share an interest in trade and the development of natural gas and oil resources and pipelines. All three would also like to encourage foreign investment to help the development of a regional infrastructure of railroads and communications.

Above all regional stability is the most important common interest sought by all the interested parties. The prevention and mediation of regional conflicts seem to be high in the agenda of the three powers. All parties appear to understand the importance of dampening the nationalism of assertive ethnic minorities or fundamentalist groupings, whether they be Azeris, Chechens, or religious movement in Tajikistan.

List of Participants

ABDURAZAKOV, Bakhodir: National Association for Friendship and Cultural Relations with Arab Countries, Tashkent

ADAMISHIN, Anatoly: Russian Ambassador, London

ADAR-SCHUTZ, Rafi: Ministry of Foreign Affairs, Jerusalem

ASULA, Mustafa: Turkish International Cooperation Agency, Ankara

ATAÖV, Türkkaya: Universities of Ankara and Bilkent, Ankara

BASHKIROV, Vassili: Embassy of the Russian Federation, London

BERGNE, Paul: Foreign and Commonwealth Office, London

BERNDORFER, Franz: Ministry of Defence, Vienna

BOISSEVAIN, Josine: Ministry of Foreign Affairs, The Hague

BURETTE, Jean-Louis: Ministry of Foreign Affairs, Brussels

von CASTELMUR, LINUS: Federal Department of Foreign Affairs, Berne

CHACALLI, George: Cyprus High Commission, London

CHARKVIANI, Gela: Chief Adviser to the Head of State on Foreign Affairs, Tbilisi

CHERNYSHEV, Albert: Ministry of Foreign Affairs, Moscow

CHRISTENSEN, Allan: Ministry of Foreign Affairs, Copenhagen

CLARK, Susan: Institute for Defense Analyses, Alexandria, Va.

DEVLET, Nadir: Marmara University, Istanbul

DUSSEX, Christian: Swiss Defence Department, Berne

EISENBARTH, Michèle: Ministry of Foreign Affairs, Luxembourg

GARMONIN, S: Ministry of Foreign Affairs, Moscow

GÖKAY, Bülent: University of Cambridge

GRANKIN, Yriy: Personal Secretary to Professor Khasbulatov, Moscow

GÉRER, Heidemaria: Federal Ministry for Foreign Affairs, Vienna

GÜRSOY, Murat: Turkish International Cooperation Agency, Ankara

HALE, William: School of Oriental and African Studies, University of London

HEATHCOTE, Mark: British Petroleum Company Ltd, London

HERZIG, Edmond: Royal Institute of International Affairs, London

HYMAN, Anthony: Central Asian Survey, London

IPEK, Kenan: Turkish Embassy, London
IVANTSOV, Petr: Embassy of the Russian Federation, London
JEKER, Rolf: Federal Ministry for Foreign Economic Affairs,
  Berne
KARAOSMANOGLU, Ali: Bilkent University, Ankara
KARAOSMANOGLU, Selim: Ministry of Foreign Affairs, Ankara
KARATSOUBA, Tatiana: Ariana SA, Geneva
KELLET, Anthony: National Defence Headquarters, Ottawa
KHASBULATOV, Ruslan: Russian Economic Academy, Moscow
KOSCHMANN, Ralf: Federal Office for Foreign and Economic
  Affairs, Berne
LALACOS, Theocharis: Embassy of Greece, Ankara
LANGHORNE, Richard: Wilton Park, Steyning
LYSKLAETT, Stig: HQ Defence Command Norway, Oslo
MAMEDIAROV, Elmar: Ministry of Foreign Affairs, Baku
MAYATSKY, Vitali: Council of the Russian Federation, Moscow
MOZAFFARI, Mehdi: Aarhus University, Aarhus
PALABIYIK, Misbah: Turkish International Cooperation Agency,
  Ankara
PARFITT, Alan: United Kingdom Delegation to the OSCE, Vienna
PAVLOV, Evgeni: Council of the Russian Federation, Moscow
PRESEL, Joseph: Department of State, Washington DC
ROBSON, Elizabeth: Foreign and Commonwealth Office, London
ROLAND, Peter: Foreign and Commonwealth Office, London
TASHAN, Seyfi: Foreign Policy Institute, Ankara
TASKENT, Kurtulus: Turkish Embassy, Almaty
TINÇ, Feraj: Hürriyet, Istanbul
TOWNSHEND, Michael: British Petroleum Exploration
  Operating Company Ltd, London
TROFIMOV, Dimitri: Centre of International Studies (MGIMO),
  Moscow
VANER, Semih: Fondation Nationale des Sciences Politiques,
  Paris
WALCZAK, Anna: Ministry of Foreign Affairs, Warsaw
WILKINSON, Richard: Foreign and Commonwealth Office,
  London
ZINGRAF, Peter: Federal Ministry of Foreign Affairs, Bonn